Glencoe Science

Chapter Resources

Electricity

Includes:

Reproducible Student Pages

ASSESSMENT
✔ Chapter Tests
✔ Chapter Review

HANDS-ON ACTIVITIES
✔ Lab Worksheets for each Student Edition Activity
✔ Laboratory Activities
✔ Foldables—Reading and Study Skills activity sheet

MEETING INDIVIDUAL NEEDS
✔ Directed Reading for Content Mastery
✔ Directed Reading for Content Mastery in Spanish
✔ Reinforcement
✔ Enrichment
✔ Note-taking Worksheets

TRANSPARENCY ACTIVITIES
✔ Section Focus Transparency Activities
✔ Teaching Transparency Activity
✔ Assessment Transparency Activity

Teacher Support and Planning
✔ Content Outline for Teaching
✔ Spanish Resources
✔ Teacher Guide and Answers

Glencoe

New York, New York   Columbus, Ohio   Chicago, Illinois   Peoria, Illinois   Woodland Hills, California

Glencoe Science

Photo Credits
Section Focus Transparency 1: D. D. Sentman/University of Alaska;
Section Focus Transparency 2: Nik Wheeler/CORBIS;
Section Focus Transparency 3: Charles O'Rear/CORBIS

Glencoe

The **McGraw·Hill** Companies

Send all inquiries to:
Glencoe/McGraw-Hill
8787 Orion Place
Columbus, OH 43240-4027

ISBN 0-07-867157-4

Printed in the United States of America.

6 7 8 9 10   079   09 08

Table of Contents

Additional Assessment Resources available with Glencoe Science:

- Exam*View*® Pro Testmaker
- Assessment Transparencies
- Performance Assessment in the Science Classroom
- Standardized Test Practice Booklet
- MindJogger Videoquizzes
- Vocabulary PuzzleMaker at **msscience.com**
- Interactive Chalkboard
- The Glencoe Science Web site at: **msscience.com**
- An interactive version of this textbook along with assessment resources are available online at: **mhln.com**

To the Teacher

This chapter-based booklet contains all of the resource materials to help you teach this chapter more effectively. Within you will find:

Reproducible pages for
- Student Assessment
- Hands-on Activities
- Meeting Individual Needs (Extension and Intervention)
- Transparency Activities

A teacher support and planning section including
- Content Outline of the chapter
- Spanish Resources
- Answers and teacher notes for the worksheets

Hands-On Activities

MiniLAB and Lab Worksheets: Each of these worksheets is an expanded version of each lab and MiniLAB found in the Student Edition. The materials lists, procedures, and questions are repeated so that students do not need their texts open during the lab. Write-on rules are included for any questions. Tables/charts/graphs are often included for students to record their observations. Additional lab preparation information is provided in the *Teacher Guide and Answers* section.

Laboratory Activities: These activities do not require elaborate supplies or extensive pre-lab preparations. These student-oriented labs are designed to explore science through a stimulating yet simple and relaxed approach to each topic. Helpful comments, suggestions, and answers to all questions are provided in the *Teacher Guide and Answers* section.

Foldables: At the beginning of each chapter there is a *Foldables: Reading & Study Skills* activity written by renowned educator, Dinah Zike, that provides students with a tool that they can make themselves to organize some of the information in the chapter. Students may make an organizational study fold, a cause and effect study fold, or a compare and contrast study fold, to name a few. The accompanying *Foldables* worksheet found in this resource booklet provides an additional resource to help students demonstrate their grasp of the concepts. The worksheet may contain titles, subtitles, text, or graphics students need to complete the study fold.

Meeting Individual Needs (Extension and Intervention)

Directed Reading for Content Mastery: These worksheets are designed to provide students with learning difficulties with an aid to learning and understanding the vocabulary and major concepts of each chapter. The *Content Mastery* worksheets contain a variety of formats to engage students as they master the basics of the chapter. Answers are provided in the *Teacher Guide and Answers* section.

Directed Reading for Content Mastery (in Spanish): A Spanish version of the *Directed Reading for Content Mastery* is provided for those Spanish-speaking students who are learning English.

Reinforcement: These worksheets provide an additional resource for reviewing the concepts of the chapter. There is one worksheet for each section, or lesson, of the chapter. The *Reinforcement* worksheets are designed to focus primarily on science content and less on vocabulary, although knowledge of the section vocabulary supports understanding of the content. The worksheets are designed for the full range of students; however, they will be more challenging for your lower-ability students. Answers are provided in the *Teacher Guide and Answers* section.

Enrichment: These worksheets are directed toward above-average students and allow them to explore further the information and concepts introduced in the section. A variety of formats are used for these worksheets: readings to analyze; problems to solve; diagrams to examine and analyze; or a simple activity or lab which students can complete in the classroom or at home. Answers are provided in the *Teacher Guide and Answers* section.

Note-taking Worksheet: The *Note-taking Worksheet* mirrors the content contained in the teacher version—*Content Outline for Teaching*. They can be used to allow students to take notes during class, as an additional review of the material in the chapter, or as study notes for students who have been absent.

Assessment

Chapter Review: These worksheets prepare students for the chapter test. The *Chapter Review* worksheets cover all major vocabulary, concepts, and objectives of the chapter. The first part is a vocabulary review and the second part is a concept review. Answers and objective correlations are provided in the *Teacher Guide and Answers* section.

Chapter Test: The *Chapter Test* requires students to use process skills and understand content. Although all questions involve memory to some degree, you will find that your students will need to discover relationships among facts and concepts in some questions, and to use higher levels of critical thinking to apply concepts in other questions. Each chapter test normally consists of four parts: Testing Concepts measures recall and recognition of vocabulary and facts in the chapter; Understanding Concepts requires interpreting information and more comprehension than recognition and recall—students will interpret basic information and demonstrate their ability to determine relationships among facts, generalizations, definitions, and skills; Applying Concepts calls for the highest level of comprehension and inference; Writing Skills requires students to define or describe concepts in multiple sentence answers. Answers and objective correlations are provided in the *Teacher Guide and Answers* section.

Transparency Activities

Section Focus Transparencies: These transparencies are designed to generate interest and focus students' attention on the topics presented in the sections and/or to assess prior knowledge. There is a transparency for each section, or lesson, in the Student Edition. The reproducible student masters are located in the *Transparency Activities* section. The teacher material, located in the *Teacher Guide and Answers* section, includes Transparency Teaching Tips, a Content Background section, and Answers for each transparency.

Teaching Transparencies: These transparencies relate to major concepts that will benefit from an extra visual learning aid. Most of these transparencies contain diagrams/photos from the Student Edition. There is one *Teaching Transparency* for each chapter. The *Teaching Transparency Activity* includes a black-and-white reproducible master of the transparency accompanied by a student worksheet that reviews the concept shown in the transparency. These masters are found in the *Transparency Activities* section. The teacher material includes Transparency Teaching Tips, a Reteaching Suggestion, Extensions, and Answers to Student Worksheet. This teacher material is located in the *Teacher Guide and Answers* section.

Assessment Transparencies: An *Assessment Transparency* extends the chapter content and gives students the opportunity to practice interpreting and analyzing data presented in charts, graphs, and tables. Test-taking tips that help prepare students for success on standardized tests and answers to questions on the transparencies are provided in the *Teacher Guide and Answers* section.

Teacher Support and Planning

Content Outline for Teaching: These pages provide a synopsis of the chapter by section, including suggested discussion questions. Also included are the terms that fill in the blanks in the students' *Note-taking Worksheets*.

Spanish Resources: A Spanish version of the following chapter features are included in this section: objectives, vocabulary words and definitions, a chapter purpose, the chapter Activities, and content overviews for each section of the chapter.

Reproducible Student Pages

Hands-On
Activities

Investigating the Electric Force

Procedure

1. Pour a layer of **salt** on a **plate**.
2. Sparingly sprinkle grains of **pepper** on top of the salt. Do not use too much pepper.
3. Rub a **rubber** or **plastic comb** on an article of **wool clothing**.
4. Slowly drag the comb through the salt and observe.

Analysis

1. How did the salt and pepper react to the comb?

   _____

   _____

   _____

2. Explain why the pepper reacted differently than the salt.

   _____

   _____

   _____

Identifying Simple Circuits

Procedure 🥽 🧤 ✋

1. The filament in a lightbulb is a piece of wire. For the bulb to light, an electric current must flow through the filament in a complete circuit. Examine the base of a **flashlight bulb** carefully. Where are the ends of the filament connected to the base?

2. Connect one piece of **wire,** a **battery,** and a flashlight bulb to make the bulb light. (There are four possible ways to do this.)

Analysis

In the space below, draw and label a diagram showing the path that is followed by the electrons in your circuit. Explain your diagram.

Current in a Parallel Circuit

Lab Preview
Directions: *Answer these questions before you begin the Lab.*

1. Why should you wear safety goggles while conducting this experiment?

_____

_____

2. What is the highest number of bulbs you will attach to the parallel circuit in this lab?

_____

The brightness of a lightbulb increases as the current in the bulb increases. In this lab you'll use the brightness of a lightbulb to compare the amount of current that flows in parallel circuits.

Real-World Question
How does connecting devices in parallel affect the electric current in a circuit?

Materials
1.5-V lightbulbs (4)
1.5-V batteries (2)
10-cm-long pieces of insulated wire (8)
battery holders (2)
minibulb sockets (4)

Goals
- **Observe** how the current in a parallel circuit changes as more devices are added.

Safety Precautions

Procedure
1. Connect one lightbulb to the battery in a complete circuit. After you've made the bulb light, disconnect the bulb from the battery to keep the battery from running down. This circuit will be the brightness tester.
2. Make a parallel circuit by connecting two bulbs as shown in Figure 1. Reconnect the bulb in the brightness tester and compare its brightness with the brightness of the two bulbs in the parallel circuit. Record your observations in the Data and Observations section.
3. Add another bulb to the parallel circuit as shown in Figure 2. How does the brightness of the bulbs change? Record your observations.
4. Disconnect one bulb in the parallel circuit. Record your observations.

Figure 1

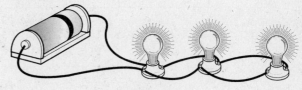

Figure 2

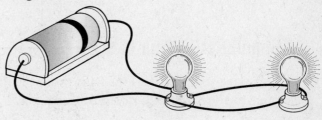

LAB (continued)

Data and Observations

Step 2 Observations

_____

_____

Step 3 Observations

_____

_____

Step 4 Observations

_____

_____

Conclude and Apply

1. **Describe** how the brightness of each bulb depends on the number of bulbs in the circuit.

_____

_____

_____

2. **Infer** how the current in each bulb depends on the number of bulbs in the circuit.

_____

_____

_____

Communicating Your Data

Compare your conclusions with those of other students in your class. **For more help, refer to the Science Skill Handbook.**

_____

_____

_____

_____

A Model for Voltage and Current

Lab Preview

Directions: *Answer these questions before you begin the Lab.*

1. What safety symbols are associated with this lab?

_____

2. What is the unit of measure of electric potential energy?

_____

> *The flow of electrons in an electric circuit is something like the flow of water in a tube connected to a water tank. By raising or lowering the height of the tank, you can increase or decrease the potential energy of the water.*

Real-World Question

How does the flow of water in a tube depend on the diameter of the tube and the height the water falls?

Materials

plastic funnel
rubber or plastic tubing of different diameters
   (1 m each)
meterstick
ring stand with ring
stopwatch
clock displaying seconds
hose clamp
binder clip
500-mL beakers (2)
Alternate materials

Goals

- **Model** the flow of current in a simple circuit.

Safety Precautions

Procedure

1. **Design** a data table in which to record your data. It should be similar to the table in your book.

2. Connect the tubing to the bottom of the funnel and place the funnel in the ring of the ring stand.

3. **Measure** the inside diameter of the rubber tubing. Record your data.

4. Place a 500-mL beaker at the bottom of the ring stand and lower the ring so the open end of the tubing is in the beaker.

5. Use the meterstick to measure the height from the top of the funnel to the bottom of the ring stand.

6. Working with a classmate, pour water into the funnel fast enough to keep the funnel full but not overflowing. Measure and record the time needed for 100 mL of water to flow into the beaker. Use the hose clamp to start and stop the flow of water.

7. Connect tubing with a different diameter to the funnel and repeat steps 2 through 6.

8. Reconnect the original piece of tubing and repeat steps 4 through 6 for several lower positions of the funnel, lowering the height by 10 cm each time.

 (continued)

Data and Observations

Analyze Your Data

1. **Calculate** the rate of flow for each trial by dividing 100 mL by the time measured for 100 mL of water to flow into the beaker.
2. **Make a graph** to show how the rate of flow depends on the funnel height.

Conclude and Apply

1. **Infer** from your graph how the rate of flow depends on the height of the funnel.

   _____

   _____

2. **Explain** how the rate of flow depends on the diameter of the tubing. Is this what you expected to happen?

   _____

   _____

   _____

3. **Identify** which of the variables you changed in your trials that corresponds to the voltage in a circuit.

   _____

   _____

4. **Identify** which of the variables you changed in your trials that corresponds to the resistance in a circuit.

   _____

   _____

5. **Infer** from your results how the current in a circuit would depend on the voltage.

   _____

   _____

   _____

6. **Infer** from your results how the current in a circuit would depend on the resistance in the circuit.

   _____

   _____

   _____

⌐ Communicating Your Data

Share your graph with other students in your class. Did other students draw the same conclusions as you? **For more help, refer to the Science Skill Handbook.**

Conductivity of Various Metals

Some materials are excellent conductors of electricity, while other materials do not conduct electricity at all. For example, metals are generally good conductors of electricity, whereas materials like wood and rubber do not conduct electricity. That is why electricians generally wear rubber gloves to protect their hands from electric shock. You will investigate how well various materials conduct electricity.

Strategy

You will determine how well different materials conduct electricity.
You will observe the behavior of a diode.

Materials

Testable Materials
aluminum foil
brass screw
copper pipe
diode
glass rod
graphite (pencil lead)
nail
paper clip
plastic pen cap
rubber eraser
wooden stick

Circuit Parts
alligator clips (2)
20-cm lengths of insulated copper wire (4)
lightbulbs (2)
lightbulb holders (2)
1.5-V batteries (2)
wire strippers

CAUTION: *Be careful working with sharp objects.*

Procedure

1. Set up a test circuit as shown in Figure 1 and described below.
2. With wire strippers, carefully scrape off 1 cm of insulation at the end of each wire.
3. Attach two wires to each of the lightbulb holders.
4. Attach one wire from each of the lightbulb holders to one exposed terminal of the batteries.
5. Leave the other wire from each lightbulb holder unattached. Attach an alligator clip to the free ends of the wires.
6. Put a lightbulb in each lightbulb holder.

Figure 1

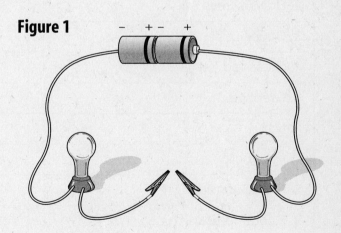

Laboratory Activity 1 (continued)

7. Before testing each material, predict whether it will allow the lightbulbs to light. Record your prediction in Table 1.
8. Test each material by attaching the alligator clips to each end as shown in Figure 2. Record your observations in Table 1
9. Reverse the direction of current in each material by switching the alligator clips. Record your observations in Table 1.
10. After testing all the materials, dismantle the circuit and place the components where instructed by your teacher.

Figure 2

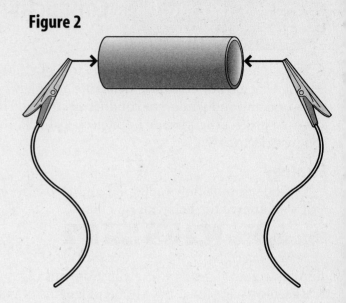

Data and Observations

Table 1

Material	Prediction before connecting	Observations when initially connected	Observations when connected in reverse
1. Aluminum foil			
2. Brass screw			
3. Copper pipe			
4. Glass rod			
5. Graphite			
6. Nail			
7. Paper clip			
8. Plastic pen cap			
9. Rubber eraser			
10. Wooden stick			
11. Diode			

Laboratory Activity 1 (continued)

Questions and Conclusions

1. From the data in Table 1, prepare a list of the materials that are conductors of electricity.

_____

_____

2. From the data in Table 1, prepare a list of materials that are not conductors.

_____

_____

3. Did any of the materials appear in both lists?

_____

_____

4. How can you tell when there is a current in the circuit?

_____

_____

_____

5. Were all of the metal materials good conductors of electricity?

_____

_____

6. Of the materials that conducted electricity, were there any nonmetals?

_____

7. Which materials would make good insulators?

_____

_____

8. How could a diode be used in a circuit?

_____

_____

Strategy Check

_____ Can you determine how well different materials conduct electricity?

_____ Can you observe the behavior of a diode?

LAB 2 Laboratory Activity

Batteries

A wet-cell battery converts chemical energy into electrical energy. Chemical reactions taking place at each of the battery terminals cause electrons to pile up at the negative terminal. Voltage is a measure of the force that causes electrons to flow from the negative terminal to the positive terminal through a conductor. The flow of charges through a conductor is current.

The amounts of voltage and current produced by a battery depend on the nature and the concentration of the chemicals in the battery. For example, a car battery produces more current and voltage than a flashlight battery does. A car battery also contains chemicals that differ in nature and concentration from the chemicals in a flashlight battery.

Strategy

You will build wet-cell batteries.
You will measure the voltage of the batteries.

Materials

250-mL beaker
aluminum foil, heavy gauge
glass rod
alligator clips (2)
copper strip

wires (2)
voltmeter
100 mL graduated cylinder
0.1 *M* hydrochloric acid

water
paper towels
vinegar
aluminum strip

Procedure

1. Line the inside of a 250-mL beaker with aluminum foil. The foil should hang over the outside edges of the beaker as shown in Figure 1.
2. Place a glass rod across the mouth of the beaker.
3. Using an alligator clip, hang a copper strip from the glass rod into the beaker. The copper strip should hang near one side of the beaker, but the copper strip should NOT touch the aluminum foil.
4. Attach a wire to the alligator clip. Then attach the other end of the wire to the positive (+) terminal of the voltmeter.
5. Attach a second alligator clip to the aluminum foil hanging over the edge of the beaker. This second alligator clip should be attached across from the copper strip as shown in Figure 1.

Figure 1

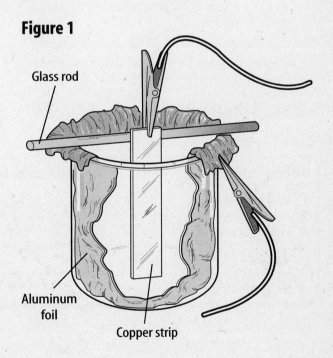

Glass rod

Aluminum foil

Copper strip

Laboratory Activity 2 (continued)

6. Attach a wire to the second alligator clip and connect the other end of this wire to the negative (−) terminal of the voltmeter as shown in Figure 2.

7. Observe the wet cell and record any changes in Table 1. Observe the voltage on the voltmeter and record it in Table 1.

8. Carefully add 75 mL of 0.1 *M* HCl to the foil-lined beaker. **CAUTION:** *HCl can cause burns. Rinse any acid spills immediately with water.*

9. After adding HCl, observe the wet cell and notice any changes to the system. Record your observations in Table 1.

10. Observe the voltage on the voltmeter and record the reading in Table 1.

11. Disconnect the wires. Under your teacher's supervision, carefully empty the acid from the beaker. Thoroughly rinse the beaker and copper strip with water and dry them with paper towels. Discard the aluminum foil.

12. Repeat steps 1 through 10 using vinegar instead of HCl. Be sure to always use new aluminum foil.

13. Repeat steps 1 through 10 using an aluminum strip instead of the copper strip. Be sure to use fresh hydrochloric acid and fresh aluminum foil.

Figure 2

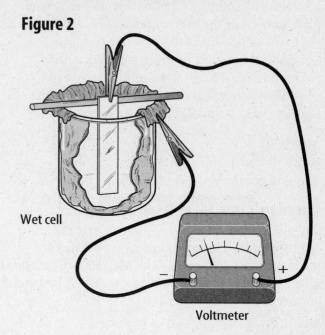

Wet cell

Voltmeter

Data and Observations

Table 1

Battery conditions	Changes to system	Voltage reading
1. Without liquid		
2. HCl, copper, aluminum		
3. Vinegar, copper, aluminum		
4. HCl, aluminum, aluminum		

Laboratory Activity 2 (continued)

Questions and Conclusions

1. From the data in Table 1, determine which battery conditions produced the largest voltage.

_____

_____

_____

2. Which liquid—HCl or vinegar—produced a higher voltage? Explain.

_____

_____

3. How do you know that a chemical reaction took place in the battery after the vinegar was added?

_____

_____

4. What metals were used to produce the batteries? How did they affect the results?

_____

_____

5. How did the effect of hydrochloric acid on the copper strip differ from its effect on the aluminum foil?

_____

_____

_____

Strategy Check

_____ Can you build a wet-cell battery?

_____ Can you measure the voltages produced by different wet-cell batteries?

Electricity

Directions: *Use this page to label your Foldable at the beginning of the chapter.*

Electricity

Electric Charge

Electric Current

Electric Circuit

a closed conducting loop

the flow of charge through a conductor

the net result of the number of protons and electrons in a body

can be positive or negative

can be series or parallel

difficulty of flow is called resistance

Meeting Individual Needs

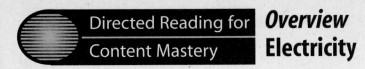

Directed Reading for Content Mastery

Overview
Electricity

Directions: *Use the following terms to complete the concept map below.*

circuit	parallel	the same
different	**$I = V/R$**	**Ohm's**

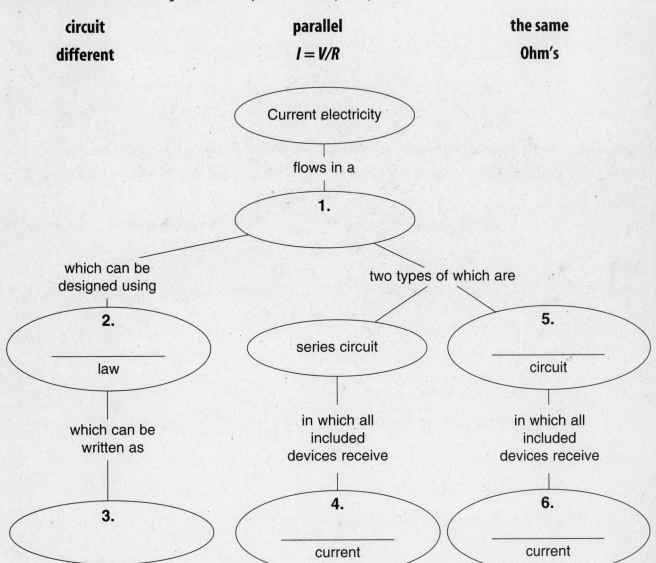

Current electricity

flows in a

1. _____

which can be designed using

two types of which are

2. _____ law

series circuit

5. _____ circuit

which can be written as

in which all included devices receive

in which all included devices receive

3. _____

4. _____ current

6. _____ current

Meeting Individual Needs

Directions: *Number the following statements so that they are in the correct order.*

_____ **7.** The boy puts his hand on the doorknob.

_____ **8.** The boy walks to the door of his room.

_____ **9.** The boy walks across the carpet.

_____ **10.** The boy feels a slight shock from static electricity.

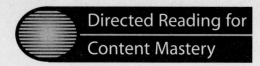

Directed Reading for Content Mastery   *Section 1* ▪ **Electric Charge**

Directions: *Place a* **C** *on the line to the left of each item that is a conductor. Place an* **I** *on the line to left of each item that is an insulator.*

_____ **1.** glass _____ **4.** wool _____ **7.** wood

_____ **2.** gold _____ **5.** copper _____ **8.** rubber

_____ **3.** plastic _____ **6.** your body _____ **9.** aluminum

Directions: *Use the figures below to mark the following statements* **T** *for true or* **F** *for false. Explain your answers. In Figure A, a charged rod is repelling a copper ball. In Figure B, two charged balls are attracted.*

Figure A

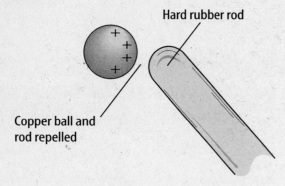

Figure B

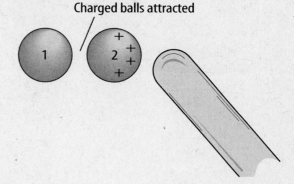

_____ **10.** In Figure A, the rod is positively charged.

_____

_____

_____ **11.** In Figure B, ball 1 has a negative charge.

_____

_____

_____ **12.** In Figure B, the positively charged rod will be attracted to ball 2.

_____

_____

Meeting Individual Needs

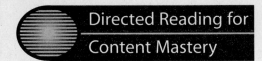

Directed Reading for
Content Mastery

Section 2 ▪ Electric Current
Section 3 ▪ Electric Circuits

Directions: *Use the diagrams to answer the questions below.* **A** *is a battery,* **B** *is a switch, and* **C** *is a lightbulb.*

Figure 1

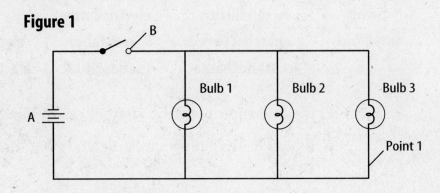

Figure 2

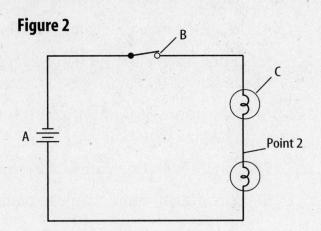

Meeting Individual Needs

1. What kind of circuit is Figure 1? _____

2. Are the lightbulbs lit in Figure 1? _____

3. If the switch was closed in Figure 1, how many of the bulbs would be lit? _____

4. If the circuit was cut at point 1, would any bulbs be lit? If so, which ones?

_____

5. What kind of circuit is Figure 2? _____

6. Are the lightbulbs lit in Figure 2? _____

7. If the circuit was cut at point 2, would either bulb be lit? _____

Directed Reading for Content Mastery

Key Terms
Electricity

Meeting Individual Needs

Directions: *Write the correct term next to its description below.*

electric field	circuit	conductors	electric current	voltage
electric force	insulators	parallel circuit	resistance	electrical power
Ohm's Law	ion	static charge	series circuit	electric discharge

_____ 1. the buildup of electric charges on an object

_____ 2. materials that allow electrons to move through them easily

_____ 3. materials through which electrons cannot move easily

_____ 4. the steady flow of electrons through a conductor

_____ 5. an unbroken path through which an electric current can flow

_____ 6. the measure of how difficult it is for electrons to flow through a material

_____ 7. a circuit with one path along which current can flow

_____ 8. a circuit with more than one path along which current can flow

_____ 9. an atom with a positive or negative charge

_____ 10. measure of how much electricity a power source can provide

_____ 11. causes charged particles to attract or repel each other

_____ 12. relationship between voltage, current, and resistance

_____ 13. area around an electric charge which is strongest closest to the charged particle

_____ 14. rate at which electrical energy is converted to another type of energy

_____ 15. rapid movement of electric charge from one place to another

Lectura dirigida para
Dominio del contenido

Sinopsis
Electricidad

Instrucciones: *Usa los siguientes términos para completar el mapa conceptual.*

circuito	**en paralelo**	**la misma**
diferente	$I = V/R$	**de Ohm**

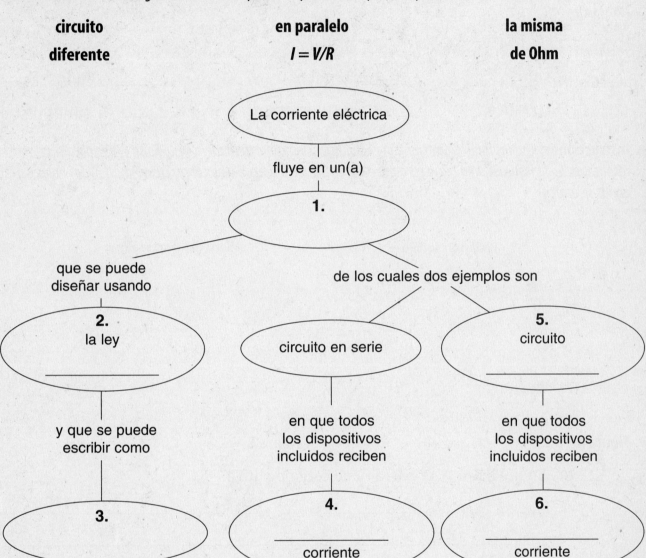

La corriente eléctrica

fluye en un(a)

1.

que se puede
diseñar usando

de los cuales dos ejemplos son

2.
la ley

_____

circuito en serie

5.
circuito

_____

y que se puede
escribir como

en que todos
los dispositivos
incluidos reciben

en que todos
los dispositivos
incluidos reciben

3.

4.

_____
corriente

6.

_____
corriente

Satisface las necesidades individuales

Instrucciones: *Enumera los siguientes enunciados y ordénalos.*

_____ **7.** El niño pone la mano en la perilla de la puerta.

_____ **8.** El niño camina hacia la puerta de su cuarto.

_____ **9.** El niño camina por la alfombra.

_____ **10.** El niño siente un choque leve de electricidad estática.

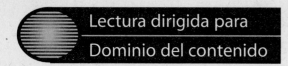

Lectura dirigida para
Dominio del contenido

Sección 1 ▪ Carga eléctrica

Instrucciones: *Escribe una* **C** *en el espacio a la izquierda de cada artículo si es u conductor. Escribe una A si es un aislante.*

_____ **1.** vidrio _____ **4.** lana _____ **7.** madera

_____ **2.** oro _____ **5.** cobre _____ **8.** hule

_____ **3.** plástico _____ **6.** tu cuerpo _____ **9.** aluminio

Instrucciones: *Usa las figuras para marcar cada afirmación como Verdadera (**V**) o Falsa (**F**). Explica tus respuestas. En la Figura A, una barra cargada está repeliendo a una bola de cobre. En la Figura B, dos bolas cargadas se atraen.*

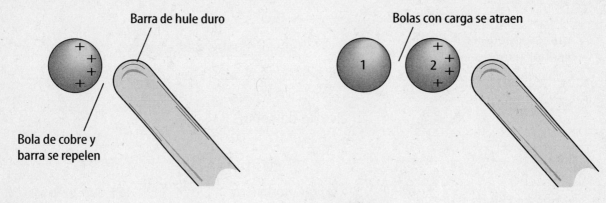

Barra de hule duro

Bola de cobre y barra se repelen

Bolas con carga se atraen

1 2

Figura A **Figura B**

_____ **10.** En la Figura A, la barra tiene carga positiva.

_____

_____

_____ **11.** En la Figura B, la bola 1 tiene carga negativa.

_____

_____

_____ **12.** En la Figura B, la barra de carga positiva será atraída por la bola 2.

_____

_____

Satisface las necesidades individuales

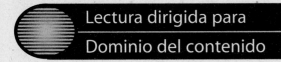

Lectura dirigida para
Dominio del contenido

Sección 2 ▪ Corriente eléctrica
Sección 3 ▪ Circuitos eléctricos

Instrucciones: *Usa los diagramas para contestar las preguntas.* **A** *es una batería,* **B** *es un interruptor y* **C** *es una bombilla.*

Figura 1

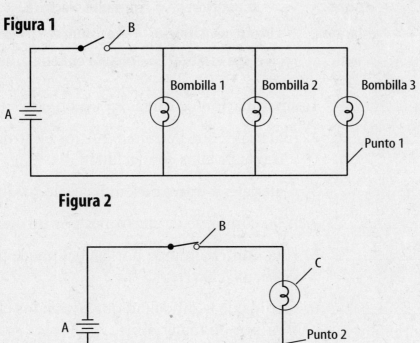

Figura 2

1. ¿Qué tipo de circuito es la Figura 1? _____

2. En la Figura 1, ¿están encendidas las bombillas? _____

3. Si en la Figura 1 se cerrara el circuito, ¿cuántas bombillas se encenderían?

_____

4. Si el circuito se cortara en el punto 1, ¿se encendería alguna bombilla?
   Si fuera así, ¿cuáles?

_____

5. ¿Qué tipo de circuito es la Figura 2? _____

6. ¿Están prendidas las bombillas en la Figura 2? _____

7. Si el circuito se cortara en el punto 2, ¿se encendería alguna bombilla?

_____

Satisface las necesidades individuales

Lectura dirigida para
Dominio del contenido

Términos claves
Electricidad

Instrucciones: *Escribe el término correcto al lado de cada descripción.*

campo eléctrico   circuito   conductores   corriente eléctrica   voltaje
fuerza eléctrica   aislantes   circuito en paralelo   resistencia   potencia eléctrica
ley de Ohm   ion   carga estática   circuito en serie   descarga eléctrica

Satisface las necesidades individuales

_____ 1. acumulación de cargas en un objeto

_____ 2. materiales que permiten que los electrones se muevan a través de ellos con facilidad

_____ 3. materiales a través de los cuales no pasan los electrones

_____ 4. flujo constante de electrones por un conductor

_____ 5. ruta ininterrumpida por la cual puede pasar una corriente eléctrica

_____ 6. medida de la dificultad que tienen los electrones de fluir por un material

_____ 7. circuito con una sola ruta por la que puede pasar la electricidad

_____ 8. circuito con más de una ruta por la que puede pasar la electricidad

_____ 9. átomo con carga positiva o negativa

_____ 10. medida de la cantidad de electricidad que una fuente puede proporcionar

_____ 11. causa que las partículas cargadas se atraigan o se repelan

_____ 12. relación entre el voltaje, la corriente y la resistencia

_____ 13. área alrededor de una carga eléctrica que es más fuerte entre más cerca esté de la partícula cargada

_____ 14. tasa a la cual la energía eléctrica se convierte en otro tipo de energía

_____ 15. movimiento rápido de una carga eléctrica de un sitio a otro

SECTION 1 | Reinforcement | Electric Charge

Directions: *Use the clues to complete the puzzle.*

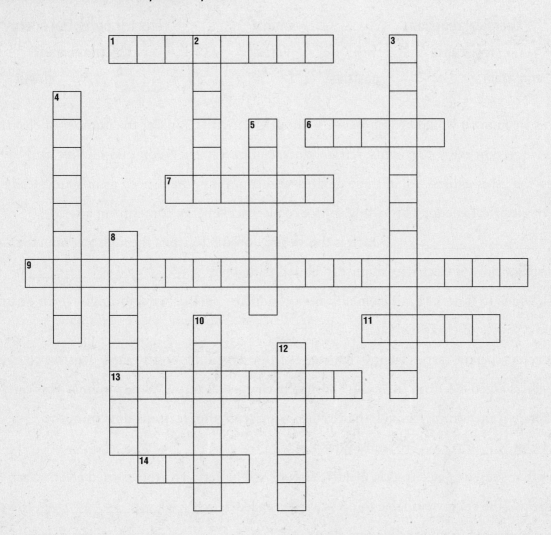

Across

1. Negatively charged atomic particle
6. Can result from touching uninsulated wire
7. Positively charged atomic particle
9. Holds protons and neutrons together in the nucleus (3 words)
11. What like charges do.
13. Something electrons cannot move through easily
14. Tiny particle of matter

Down

2. Metal used for electrical wire
3. Gets stronger as you get closer to an electric charge (2 words)
4. Something electrons move through easily
5. What opposite charges do
8. Charge of an atom that has lost electrons
10. Atomic particle that has no charge
12. Buildup of electric charges

Meeting Individual Needs

SECTION
2 Reinforcement **Electric Current**

Directions: *Complete the paragraphs using the terms listed below.*

chemical reactions	**ohms**	**electric potential energy**
resistance	**volts**	**electric current**
negative	**positive**	**V**	**circuit**

Life as we know it would be impossible without electricity. Think of the number of electrical devices we rely on every day: lights, refrigerators, computers, televisions, flashlights, car headlights, watches–the list is endless. All of these devices, and countless others, need a constant, steady source of electrical energy. This steady source of electrical energy comes from a(n) **1.** _____, which is the steady flow of electrons through a conductor.

This steady flow of electricity requires a closed path, or **2.** _____, through which to flow. Its basic elements are a conductor, such as wire, through which electrons flow and a source of electrons, such as a battery.

An electric current carries energy that comes from separating positive and negative charges. Negatively charged electrons "seek out" positively charged electrons to recombine. This can only happen if they travel through the circuit. In a circuit, the electrons flow from the **3.** _____ end to the **4.** _____ end.

A familiar source of electrons in electric circuits is a battery. The total stored electrical energy in a battery—the energy available to do work—is called **5.** _____. This energy is measured in units called **6.** _____, which is abbreviated **7.** _____. Batteries rely on **8.** _____ to separate positive and negative electrical charges. When the negative and positive ends of the charges are connected by a conductor, a circuit forms and the electrical energy is available to do work.

However, the electrons don't flow completely freely through the circuit. Depending on the material used for the conductor, the electrons have more or less difficulty flowing. The measure of how difficult it is for electrons to flow through a circuit is called **9.** _____. This is measured in units called **10.** _____.

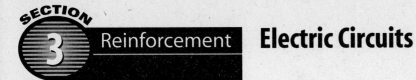

Electric Circuits

Directions: *Use the terms and statements from the list below to complete the table.*

kilowatt   amount of electric energy used by a device

series: a circuit that has only one path for the electric current to follow

Ohm's law   power = current × voltage   series circuit

parallel: a circuit that has more than one path for the electric current to follow

watt   voltage = current × resistance   kW

$P = I \times V$ parallel circuit $V = I \times R$ W

Important Facts About Electric Circuits	
1. There is a relationship among voltage, current, and resistance in an electric circuit.	
a. Name of law:	
b. Expression of law:	
c. Equation:	
2. There are two types of electric circuits.	
a. Two types of circuits:	(1) (2)
b. Definitions of these circuits:	(1) (2)
3. The electrical power of a circuit can be measured.	
a. Definition of electrical power:	
b. Unit of electrical power:	(1) Name: (2) Abbreviation: (3) Term for 1000 units: (4) Abbreviation for 1000 units:
c. Determining the electrical power of a circuit:	(1) Expression: (2) Formula:

Enrichment **Lightning Varieties**

Meeting Individual Needs

Lightning is one of nature's most spectacular phenomena. It is also one of the most common. At any given moment, about 2,000 thunderstorms take place around the world. In the United States, lightning strikes hit millions of points every year.

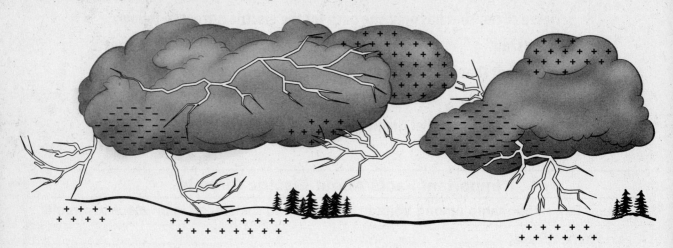

The most familiar lightning bolts are *cloud-to-ground lightning*. The bottom of the cloud is negatively charged, while the ground is positively charged. Static energy moves from the bottom of the cloud to the ground in sections called *step-leaders*. That's why the bolts appear jagged. As a step-leader gets close to the ground, a positively charged bolt called a *leader* flashes up from the ground to meet it. This is *ground-to-cloud lightning*.

The most common lightning doesn't hit the ground. Lightning that goes between sections of a cloud is called *intracloud lightning*.

It redistributes energy between positive and negative areas in the same cloud. Usually, an intracloud lightning bolt is not visible. Instead it looks like a broad flash in the sky and is often called *sheet lightning*.

Lightning between oppositely charged areas of different clouds is called *cloud-to-cloud lightning*. Lightning can also move from a cloud to a charged air pocket. This lightning is called *cloud-to-air lightning*.

Lightning can discharge 100 million volts of electricity and reach temperatures of over 33,000°C.

1. What are the common features of all of these forms of lightning?

   _____

   _____

   _____

2. Why are we usually unaware of ground-to-cloud lightning?

   _____

   _____

SECTION 2 Enrichment

How much electricity do you use?

Janet and Jonas are working on a budget. To plan on costs for electricity, they gathered information about how much energy their appliances use in a year. The information they used is listed in the table. Then they investigated the electric power supplier to learn more about costs. The chart to the right lists Janet and Jonas's common household appliances and how much electricity they use in one year. The electric company bills people for the amount of electricity they use, based on a unit called the kilowatt-hour. A kilowatt-hour equals the amount of energy produced by one kilowatt of power in one hour.

Appliance	Kilowatt-hours used per year
Dishwasher	363
Microwave oven	190
Toaster	39
Washing machine	103
Clothes dryer	933
Vacuum cleaner	46
Hair dryer	14
Color television	440

Meeting Individual Needs

1. Imagine that the electric company charges $0.13 for a kilowatt-hour. Calculate how much each of these appliance would cost Janet and Jonas per month.

   a. Doing the laundry _____

   b. Using the microwave oven _____

   c. Vacuuming the house _____

   d. Watching television _____

   e. Running the dishwasher _____

2. Find out how much electricity costs in your area by checking a recent bill or by calling your electric company. Then calculate your family's yearly cost for each of the items above.

_____

_____

_____

_____

_____

_____

_____

SECTION 3 Enrichment

To Resist or Not to Resist

Meeting Individual Needs

Georg Ohm was a German physicist born in 1787. He is most famous for his work studying the resistance of materials to electric current.

Ohm discovered the relationship between an electric current and the materials through which it passes. He learned that the amount of steady current that passes through a material is directly proportional to the potential difference (voltage) and inversely proportional to the resistance of that material. In 1827 he established that resistance for a circuit was generally constant at a fixed temperature.

Ohm's Law

Ohm's law states that resistance is equal to the electromotive force, measured in potential difference, or volts (V), divided by the current, measured in amperes (I). In other words, R=V/I.

The unit of measure for electrical resistance is named after George Ohm. The ohm is equal to the resistance that allows one amphere (I) to flow through one volt (V).

Applies to Alternating Current

Ohm's law not only applies to direct current circuits, but with modification, to alternating currents as well. With alternating current, the current varies, so in addition to resistance, another form of opposition arises, called reactance. Resistance combined with reactance forms impedance.

Electricians apply Ohm's law when calculating the efficiency of a circuit. They can determine how components such as capacitors, transistors, and connecting wires will affect current flow.

1. What is the current through a 40-ohm resistance that has a potential difference of 160 volts?

_____

_____

2. If the headlight on your mom's car has a resistance of 32 ohms and the car battery put out 12 V, what is the current through the headlight circuit?

_____

_____

3. The motor for your electric car is attached to a generator. The motor has a resistance of 28 ohms and the current is 3.8 amperes (A). What is the generator's voltage?

_____

_____

4. If a clock radio uses 2×10^{-4} A of current when you run it on a 3-V battery, what resistance is its circuit providing?

_____

_____

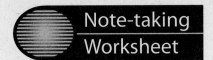 **Note-taking Worksheet** **Electricity**

Section 1   Electric Charge

A. Electricity begins at the _____ level where protons and electrons have electric charge.

  1. _____ carry a positive change.

  2. Electrons carry a _____ charge.

  3. _____ form when atoms lose or gain electrons and become positively or negatively charged.

  4. Electrons can move from object to object; _____ is the buildup of electric charge on an object.

  5. A flow of charge can be caused by ions moving in a _____.

B. All objects exert an _____ _____ on each other; it can be attractive or repulsive.

  1. Like charges repel, unlike charges _____.

  2. Electric charges exert a force on each other at a distance through an _____ _____ which exists around every electric charge.

C. _____—material which does not allow electrons to move easily; _____—material that allows electrons to move easily; metals are the best conductors.

D. _____ _____—rapid movement of excess charge from one place to another; lightning is an electric discharge.

E. _____—provides a pathway to drain excess charge into the Earth; lightning rods provide grounding for many buildings.

Section 2   Electric Current

A. _____ _____—flow of charge through a conductor

  1. In solids the flowing charges are _____; in liquids the flowing charges are positive or negative ions.

    a. _____—closed conducting loop through which electric currents continuously flow

Meeting Individual Needs

Note-taking Worksheet (continued)

Meeting Individual Needs

    b. Current _____ can do work in an electric device; it carries electrical energy through wire.

    c. _____—measure of how much electric energy an electron in a circuit can gain from a battery.

    d. Electrons move in a circuit and have millions and millions of _____.

  2. The voltage of a battery depends on the amount and type of _____ used to create the chemical reactions in a battery.

  3. Batteries _____ when the original chemicals are used up and the chemical reactions in the battery stop.

B. _____—measure of how difficult it is for electrons to flow through a material

  1. Insulators generally have much _____ resistance then conductors.

  2. The amount of electric energy that is converted into thermal energy _____ as the resistance of wire increases.

  3. The length and _____ of a wire affect electron flow.

Section 3   Electric Circuits

A. The amount of current is determined by the _____ supplied by a battery and the resistance of the conductor.

  1. As the resistance in an electric current increases, the current in the circuit _____.

  2. _____—current = voltage/resistance

  3. When the voltage in a circuit increases, the _____ increases.

B. There are _____ kinds of basic circuits: series and parallel.

  1. A _____ **circuit** has only one path for the electric current to follow—if the path is broken, the current will no longer flow and all devices in the circuit stop working.

  2. A _____ **circuit** has more than one path for the electric current to follow.

C. For safety, circuits in homes and buildings have _____ or circuit breakers that limit the amount of current in the wiring.

Note-taking Worksheet (continued)

D. _____ _____—rate at which an appliance converts electrical

energy to another form of energy

1. Power = current × voltage

2. The unit of power is the _____.

3. Electric companies charge customers for the number of _____ they use in

a month.

E. Electricity can be _____.

1. Current can enter your body and shock you when your body accidentally becomes part of

an electric circuit.

2. Lightning can be deadly; if caught outdoors near lightning use lightning-safety precautions.

Assessment

Chapter Review

Electricity

Part A. Vocabulary Review

Directions: *Use the clues to complete the puzzle.*

Across

2. Circuit with more than one path

4. A material that current does not easily flow through

8. Rapid movement of excess electrons from one place to another (2 words)

11. Rate at which electric energy is converted to another form (2 words)

12. Closed path through which current can flow

13. Buildup of electric charges in one place (2 words)

Down

1. Exists around every electric charge (2 words)

3. Steady flow of electrons (2 words)

5. Circuit with only one path

6. Relationship between voltage, current, and resistance (2 words)

7. Measure of how difficult it is for electrons to flow

9. A material that current flows through easily

10. Measure of electrical potential energy

Chapter Review (continued)

Part B. Concept Review

Directions: *Fill in the blanks with the correct terms.*

1. An object becomes positively charged if it _____.

2. Objects with unlike charges _____ each other.

3. The farther you get from an electric charge, the _____ the electric field.

4. When an object is grounded, it becomes electrically _____.

5. A simple circuit consists of a conductor, wires, and _____.

6. As energy carried by a current increases, _____ increases.

7. Electric energy can be stored by _____ charges.

8. In a battery, electrons flow from the _____ terminal to the _____ terminal.

9. When a wire is made thicker, its resistance _____.

10. The unit used to measure electric current is the _____.

11. According to Ohm's law, voltage = _____ × _____.

12. If a 1.5-V battery is connected in a simple circuit to a lightbulb with a resistance of 8 ohms, the amount of current flowing through the circuit is _____.

13. In a series circuit, each device that is added to the circuit decreases the _____.

14. If you multiply the voltage in a circuit by the current, you are finding the _____ of the circuit.

15. Electric energy usage on your electric bill is measured in _____.

Directions: *Answer the following questions on the lines provided.*

16. How are series and parallel circuits similar? How are they different?

_____

_____

_____

_____

17. What are two ways an electric shock can harm the body?

_____

_____

_____

Assessment

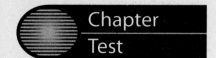

Electricity

Chapter Test

I. Testing Concepts

Directions: *For each of the following, write the letter of the term that best completes the statement.*

_____ 1. _____ is an example of a good electrical insulator.
  a. Aluminum foil   **b.** Silver   **c.** Copper   **d.** Rubber

_____ 2. If an object loses electrons, the object will have a _____ change.
  a. positive   **b.** static   **c.** neutral   **d.** negative

_____ 3. A simple complete circuit must have wires connected to a(n) _____.
  a. switch   **c.** source of electrons
  b. switch and a conductor   **d.** source of electrons and a conductor

_____ 4. A battery produces current electricity from _____.
  a. mechanical energy   **c.** chemical energy
  b. static electricity   **d.** strong nuclear force

_____ 5. When you walk across a carpeted floor and then touch a metal doorknob, the "shock" you may feel occurs because of a(n) _____.
  a. static discharge   **c.** static charge
  b. electric field   **d.** chemical reaction

_____ 6. A measure of the potential energy available in a complete circuit is _____.
  a. current   **b.** power   **c.** resistance   **d.** voltage

_____ 7. Dry skin is a good _____.
  a. conductor   **c.** source of negative charges
  b. insulator   **d.** source of positive charges

_____ 8. The negative terminal of a battery has _____.
  a. a pileup of positive charges   **c.** a pileup of negative charges
  b. a positive charge   **d.** no charge

_____ 9. To prevent overloading in a parallel circuit, you could install a(n) _____.
  a. power meter   **c.** electric generator
  b. fuse   **d.** ground

_____ 10. When you rub a balloon on your hair, _____ go from your hair to the balloon.
  a. electrons   **b.** protons   **c.** atoms   **d.** neutrons

_____ 11. The filament in a light bulb is often made from tungsten wire because tungsten is a _____.
  a. good conductor and has a high resistance
  b. good conductor and has a low resistance
  c. good insulator and has a high resistance
  d. good insulator and has a low resistance

Assessment

Chapter Test (continued)

_____ 12. In a battery, electrons flow from _____.
   a. one positive terminal to the other positive terminal
   b. the positive terminal to the negative terminal
   c. the negative terminal to the positive terminal
   d. one negative terminal to the other negative terminal

_____ 13. A wire that is _____ would have the greatest electrical resistance.
   a. short and thick   c. long and thick
   b. short and thin   d. long and thin

_____ 14. According to Ohm's law, _____.
   a. current = voltage × resistance   c. voltage = current × resistance
   b. power = current × voltage   d. resistance = current × power

_____ 15. Two identical balloons are both rubbed with wool. If the balloons are brought near each other, they will _____.
   a. attract each other   c. have no effect on each other
   b. repel each other   d. ground each other

_____ 16. When you use an electric appliance, the amount of electric energy used depends _____.
   a. only on the appliance's power
   b. only on how long it is used
   c. on both the appliance's power and how long it is used
   d. on the appliance's power but not how long it is used

_____ 17. A series circuit is a circuit with _____ path(s) for the electric current to follow.
   a. no   b. one   c. more than one   d. infinite

Directions: *List the units used to measure each of the following.*

18. power of a microwave oven

_____

19. strength of a battery

_____

20. current flowing through a circuit

_____

21. resistance of a wire

_____

Assessment

Chapter Test (continued)

II. Understanding Concepts

Skill: Recognizing Cause and Effect

Directions: *Read the following statements, then fill in the missing cause or effect in the table below.*

Nylon cloth loses electrons to rubber. A rubber rod is rubbed with a nylon cloth and then brought near a table tennis ball that is suspended on a string.

Cause	Effect
1.	The nylon cloth has a positive charge.
2. The rod is rubbed with nylon.	
3.	The ball is attracted to the rod.
4. The ball is also rubbed with the nylon cloth.	
5. The rod is brought near the ball.	

Skill: Interpreting Scientific Illustrations

Directions: *Answer the following questions on the lines provided.*

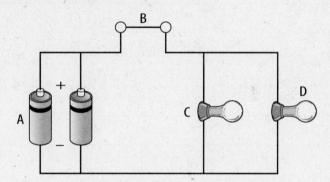

6. Identify each of the following parts of the circuit shown above.

   A. _____

   B. _____

   C. _____

7. Is the circuit a series or parallel circuit?

   _____

8. If C is removed, how will D be affected?

   _____

Chapter Test (continued)

III. Applying Concepts

Directions: *Study the diagrams, then answer the questions that follow.*

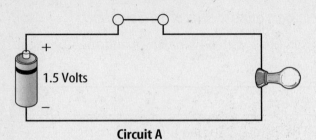

Circuit A   **Circuit B**

1. If the bulb in circuit A has a resistance of 0.75 ohms, calculate the current in the circuit.

_____

_____

2. What is the total voltage in circuit B?

_____

3. If the current in circuit B is 4 amperes, calculate the power of the bulb in circuit B.

_____

_____

4. If the bulbs in circuits A and B are identical, which bulb would burn brighter? Explain.

_____

_____

_____

IV. Writing Skills

Directions: *Answer the following questions using complete sentences.*

1. What is the purpose of placing metal lightning rods at the top of tall buildings?

_____

_____

_____

2. A person who has grasped a current-carrying wire might not be able to let go. Why?

_____

_____

_____

Transparency
Activities

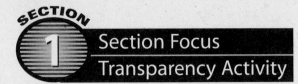

SECTION 1 Section Focus
Transparency Activity

A Spritely Vision

The lightning that we usually see is below the clouds, but there is activity high above the clouds, too. These events have some pretty fanciful names, like sprites, elves, and blue jets. This photo shows the red flash of a sprite, which sometimes occurs during thunderstorms.

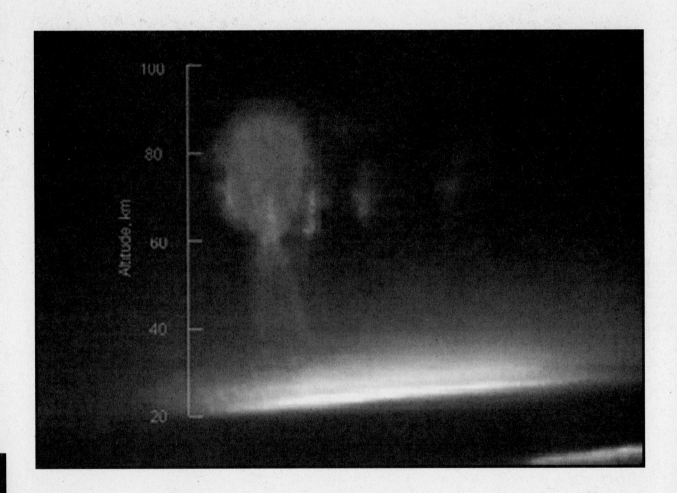

1. What is lightning?

2. How does this sprite appear similar to lightning? Different?

3. How is a flash of lightning different from a glowing lightbulb?

Transparency Activities

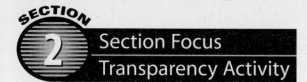

Go with the Flow!

Highways in heavily used areas are designed with many lanes to keep traffic moving, but sometimes it doesn't work.

1. Describe what is happening in the picture. What would traffic be like if there were the same number of cars but fewer lanes? What would traffic be like if there were the same number of cars but twice as many lanes?

2. How might the flow of traffic on a road be like the flow of electricity in a wire?

Transparency Activities

Section Focus Transparency Activity

In the Chips

A few decades ago, a single computer was the size of a classroom. Today's laptops, however, are smaller, faster, and have more memory. Much of this change is due to the development of microcircuits like the silicon chip in this photo.

1. *Micro* means small or minute. What advantages do very small circuits offer?

2. List three things that you use every day that have a circuit.

3. Which items in your home do you think use the most electricity?

Transparency Activities

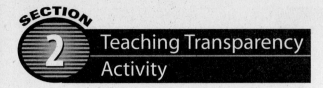

SECTION 2 — Teaching Transparency Activity

Flowing Current

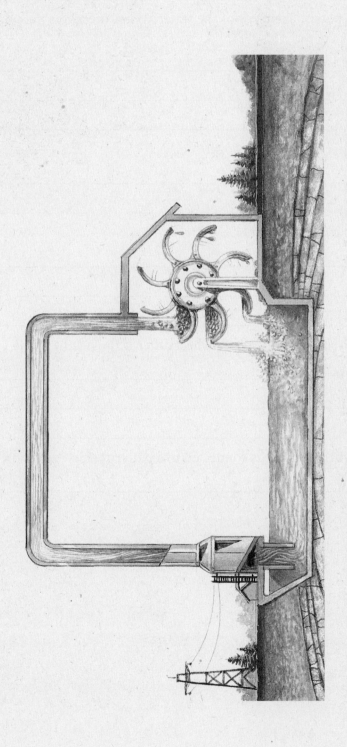

Teaching Transparency Activity (continued)

1. How is the potential energy of the water increased?

   _____

   _____

2. What measures the potential energy of the water? What measures the potential energy of electric current?

   _____

   _____

   _____

3. What causes the water wheel to do work?

   _____

   _____

4. How does electric current transfer energy?

   _____

   _____

   _____

5. How would the movement of the water wheel differ if the height of the pipes were increased?

   _____

   _____

   _____

6. What is a circuit? When a circuit is connected to a battery, which direction do the electrons flow?

   _____

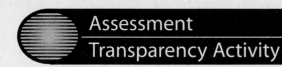

Electricity

Assessment Transparency Activity

Directions: *Carefully review the table and answer the following questions.*

Approximate Cost of Electricity for Some Appliances			
Appliance	Wattage	Average daily use (hours)	Approximate cost per month
Air cleaner	35	24	$2.00
Box fan	100	24	$5.75
Clothes dryer	5,000	1/2	$6.00
Color TV (19 inch)	70	6	$1.05
Personal computer	150	8	$2.90
Laser printer	70	2	$0.30

1. Which of the listed appliances costs the most to operate each month?
   A Box fan
   B Personal computer
   C Clothes dryer
   D Color TV

2. According to the table, if two appliances are used for the same number of hours, the one with higher wattage will cost ___.
   F more to operate
   G less to operate
   H the same to operate
   J can't answer from table

3. The color TV costs more to operate than the laser printer because ___.
   A the wattage of the color TV is higher
   B the color TV is on longer
   C the color TV is bigger
   D the power company charges more for TVs

Teacher Support and Planning

Teacher Support and Planning

 Content Outline for Teaching

Electricity

Section 1   Electric Charge

Underlined words and phrases are to be filled in by students on the Note-taking Worksheet.

A. Electricity begins at the <u>atomic</u> level where protons and electrons have electric charge.

1. **Protons** carry a positive change.

2. Electrons carry a <u>negative</u> charge.

3. **Ions** form when atoms lose or gain electrons and become positively or negatively charged.

4. Electrons can move from object to object; <u>static charge</u> is the buildup of electric charge on an object.

5. A flow of charge can be caused by ions moving in a <u>solution</u>.

B. All objects exert an **electric force** on each other; it can be attractive or repulsive.

1. Like charges repel, unlike charges <u>attract</u>.

2. Electric charges exert a force on each other at a distance through an **electric field** which exists around every electric charge

C. **Insulator**—material which does not allow electrons to move easily; **conductor**—material that allows electrons to move easily; metals are the best conductors

D. **Electric discharge**—rapid movement of excess charge from one place to another; lightning is an electric discharge.

E. <u>Grounding</u>—provides a pathway to drain excess charge into the Earth; lightning rods provide grounding for many buildings.

DISCUSSION QUESTION:
What is static charge? *Buildup of electric charge on an object*

Section 2   Electric Current

A. **Electric current** – flow of charge through a conductor

  1. In solids the flowing charges are electrons; in liquids the flowing charges are positive or negative ions.

      a. **Circuit**—closed conducting loop through which electric currents continuously flow

      b. Current flow can do work in an electric device; flow carries electrical energy through wire.

      c. **Voltage**—measure of how much electric energy an electron in a circuit can gain from a battery.

      d. Electrons move in a circuit and have millions and millions of collisions.

  2. The voltage of a battery depends on the amount and type of chemicals used to create the chemical reactions in a battery.

  3. Batteries die when the original chemicals are used up and the chemical reactions in the battery stop.

B. **Resistance**—measure of how difficult it is for electrons to flow through a material

  1. Insulators generally have much higher resistance then conductors.

  2. The amount of electric energy that is converted into thermal energy increases as the resistance of wire increases.

  3. The length and thickness of a wire affect electron flow.

DISCUSSION QUESTION:
Why do batteries die? *The chemicals providing the source of chemical reactions are used up.*

Section 3   Electric Circuits

A. The amount of current is determined by the voltage supplied by a battery and the resistance of the conductor.

  1. As the resistance in an electric current increases, the current in the circuit decreases.

  2. **Ohm's law**—current = voltage/resistance

  3. When the voltage in a circuit increases, the current increases.

B. There are two kinds of basic circuits: series and parallel.

  1. A **series circuit** has only one path for the electric current to follow—if the path is broken, the current will no longer flow and all devices in the circuit stop working.

Content Outline for Teaching (continued)

    2. A **parallel** **circuit** has more than one path for the electric current to follow.

C. For safety, circuits in homes and buildings have <u>fuses</u> or circuit breakers that limit the amount of current in the wiring.

D. <u>**Electric power**</u>—rate at which an appliance converts electrical energy to another form of energy

    1. Power = current × voltage

    2. The unit of power is the <u>watt</u>.

    3. Electric companies charge customers for the number of <u>kilowatt-hours</u> they use in a month.

E. Electricity can be <u>dangerous</u>.

    1. Current can enter your body and shock you when your body accidentally becomes part of an electric circuit.

    2. Lightning can be deadly; if caught outdoors near lightning use lightning-safety precautions.

DISCUSSION QUESTION:
How does the body receive an electric shock? *The body becomes part of an electric circuit; ions in the body conduct charge.*

Electricidad

① Carga eléctrica

Lo que aprenderás

- A describir como es que los objetos se cargan eléctricamente.
- A explicar como es que las cargas eléctricas afectan a otras cargas eléctricas.
- A diferenciar entre aisladores y conductores.
- A describir como es que ocurren las descargas eléctricas tales como los rayos.

Vocabulario

ion / ion: partícula con carga que posee o más o menos electrones que protones.

static charge / carga estática: acumulación de cargas eléctricas en un objeto.

electric force / fuerza eléctrica: fuerza de atracción o de repulsión que ejercen todos los objetos con carga.

electric field / campo eléctrico: campo a través del cual las cargas eléctricas ejercen una fuerza mutua.

insulator / aislador: material a través del cual no pueden fluir los electrones fácilmente; por ejemplo, la madera o el vidrio.

conductor / conductor: material, como el cobre o la plata, a través del cual los electrones se pueden desplazar fácilmente.

electric discharge / descarga eléctrica: movimiento rápido del exceso de carga de un lugar a otro.

¿Por que es importante?

Todo el fenómeno eléctrico resulta del comportamiento de cargas eléctricas.

② Corriente eléctrica

Lo que aprenderás

- A relacionar voltaje a la energía eléctrica que lleva la corriente eléctrica
- A describir una batería y como es que produce corriente eléctrica.
- A explicar resistencias eléctricas.

Vocabulario

electric current / corriente eléctrica: flujo de corriente, ya sea un flujo de electrones o de iones, a través de un conductor.

circuit / circuito: bucle conductor cerrado por donde puede fluir la corriente eléctrica.

voltage / voltaje: una medida de la cantidad de energía eléctrica que tiene cada electrón en una batería; se mide en voltios (V).

resistance / resistencia: una medida del grado de dificultad con que los electrones pueden fluir a través de un material; la unidad de medida es el omnio (Ω).

Por qué es importante

Los aparatos eléctricos que usas, dependen de corriente eléctrica.

③ Circuitos eléctricos

Lo que aprenderás

- A explicar cómo se relacionan el voltaje, la corriente y la resistencia en un circuito.
- A investigar la diferencia entre los circuitos en serie y en paralelo.
- A determinar la potencia eléctrica utilizada en un circuito.
- A describir como evitar un peligroso choque eléctrico.

Vocabulario

Ohm's law / ley de Ohm: relación entre el voltaje, la corriente y la resistencia en un circuito.

series circuit / circuito en serie: circuito con una sola trayectoria a través de la cual puede fluir la corriente eléctrica.

parallel circuit / circuito paralelo: circuito que tiene más de una trayectoria para el flujo de la corriente eléctrica.

electric power / potencia eléctrica: tasa a la cual un artefacto eléctrico convierte la energía eléctrica en otra forma de energía; su uso se mide en kilovatios-hora con contadores de electricidad.

Por qué es importante

Los circuitos eléctricos controlan el flujo de corriente eléctrica en todos los aparatos eléctricos.

 ## Corriente en un circuito paralelo

La intensidad del brillo de los bombillos aumenta o se reduce a medida que más o menos corriente fluye a través de él. En este laboratorio usarás el brillo de los bombillos para comparar la cantidad de corriente que fluye en circuitos paralelos.

Materiales

4 bombillos de 1.5 V
2 baterías de 1.5 V
8 pedazos de alambre aislado de 10 cm de largo
2 sostenedores de baterías
4 receptáculos para bombillos pequeños

Preguntas del mundo real

¿Cómo afecta la conexión en paralelo de aparatos a la corriente eléctrica de un circuito?

Meta

- **Observa** la manera en que la corriente eléctrica de un circuito cambia a medida que se agregan aparatos.

Medidas de seguridad

Procedimiento

1. Conecta un bombillo a una batería en un circuito completo. Después de que hayas prendido el bombillo, desconecta el bombillo de la batería para evitar que la batería se descargue. Este circuito será el probador de brillantez.
2. Haz un circuito paralelo conectando dos bombillos como se muestra en el diagrama. Reconecta el bombillo en el probador de brillantez y compara esta con la brillantez de los dos bombillos del circuito en paralelo. Registra tus observaciones.
3. Agrega otro bombillo al circuito en paralelo como se muestra en la figura. ¿Cómo cambia la brillantez de los bombillos?
4. Desconecta un bombillo del circuito paralelo.

Concluye y aplica

1. **Describe** cómo las brillantes de cada bombilla de luz depende del número de bombillas en el circuito.
2. **Infiere** cómo la corriente en cada una de las bombillas de luz depende del número de bombillas en el circuito.

 ## Un modelo para el voltaje y la corriente

El flujo de electrones en un circuito eléctrico es similar al flujo de agua. Al elevar o bajar la altura de un tanque de agua, puedes incrementar o reducir la energía potencial del agua.

Preguntas del mundo real

¿Cómo se ve afectado el flujo de agua que pasa por un tubo al variar la altura de un recipiente de agua y el diámetro del tubo?

Materiales

embudo de plástico
tubería de caucho o plástico de diferentes
    diámetros (1 m cada uno)
regla de un metro
soporte con aro de metal
cronómetro
*reloj con segundero
grapa para manguera
*grapa de escritorio
2 vasos de precipitados de 500 mL
*Materiales alternativos

Meta

- Modelar el flujo de corriente en un circuito simple.

Medidas de seguridad

Procedimiento

1. **Diseña** una tabla de datos para anotar tus datos. Debe ser similar a la tabla de la págin anterior.
2. Conecta la tubería al extremo inferior del embudo y coloca el embudo en el aro de metal de soporte.

3. **Mide** el diámetro interior de la tubería de plástico. Anota tus datos.
4. Coloca el vaso de precipitados de 500 mL al fondo del soporte y debajo de anillo de metal de manera que el extremo abierto de la tubería esté en el vaso de precipitado.
5. Usa la vara de medir para medir la altura desde la parte superior del embudo hasta la parte inferior del soporte.
6. Trabaja con un compañero, vierte agua dentro del embudo lo suficientemente rápido para mantener el embudo lleno sin derramarlo. Mide y anota el tiempo que necesitan 100 mL de agua para fluir dentro del vaso de precipitados. Usa la grapa para manguera para iniciar y detener el flujo del agua.
7. Conecta tuberías de diferentes diámetros al embudo y repite los pasos del 2 al 6.
8. Reconecta la tubería original y repite los pasos del 4 al 6 con el embudo en varias posiciones más bajas, disminuyendo la altura 10 cm cada vez.

Analiza tus datos

1. **Calcula** la tasa de flujo para cada caso dividiendo 100 mL por el tiempo que toma que 100 mL de agua llenen el vaso de precipitado.
2. Haz un gráfica que muestre cómo la tasa del flujo depende de la altura del embudo.

Concluye y aplica

1. **Infiere** de tu gráfica cómo la tasa del flujo depende de la altura del embudo.
2. **Explica** cómo la tasa del flujo depende del diámetro de la tubería. ¿Era eso lo que esperabas que suceda?
3. **Identifica** cuál de las variables que cambiaste en tus intentos corresponden al voltaje en un circuito.
4. **Identifica** cuál de las variables que cambiaste corresponden a la resistencia.
5. **Infiere** de tus resultados cómo la corriente de un circuito depende del voltaje.
6. **Infiere** de tus resultados cómo la corriente de un circuito depende de la resistencia en el circuito.

Guía de estudio

Repasa las ideas principales

Refiérete a las figuras de tu libro de texto.

Sección 1 Carga eléctrica

1. Los dos tipos de cargas eléctricas son positiva y negativa. Cargas iguales se rechazan y cargas diferentes se atraen.
2. Un objeto carga negativamente si gana electrones y positivamente si pierde electrones.
3. Los objetos cargados eléctricamente tienen un campo eléctrico que los rodea y ejercen una fuerza eléctrica entre ellos.
4. Los electrones se pueden mover con facilidad a través de conductores, pero no tan fácilmente a través de aislantes.

Sección 2 Corriente eléctrica

1. La corriente eléctrica es el flujo de cargas, generalmente de electrones o iones.
2. La energía que los electrones transportan en un circuito aumenta a medida que aumenta el voltaje en el circuito.
3. Una batería provee una fuente de corriente eléctrica al usar reacciones químicas para separar cargas positivas y negativas.
4. A medida que los electrones fluyen en un circuito, algo de su energía eléctrica se pierde debido a la resistencia en el circuito.

Teacher Support & Planning

Sección 3 Circuitos eléctricos

1. En un circuito eléctrico, el voltaje, la corriente y la resistencia están relacionadas por la ley de Ohm, que se expresa como $V = I \times R$.

2. Los tipos básicos de circuitos eléctricos son circuitos paralelos y circuitos en serie. Un circuito en serie tiene sólo una trayectoria para la corriente eléctrica, pero un circuito paralelo tiene más de una trayectoria.

3. La tasa a la que los artefactos eléctricos usan energía eléctrica es la potencia eléctrica que usa el artefacto. Las compañías eléctricas les cobran a los clientes por el uso de la energía eléctrica en unidades de kilovatios-horas.

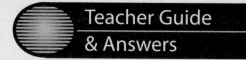

Hands-On Activities

MiniLAB: Try at Home (page 3)
1. The comb attracted the pepper flakes and some small crystals of salt.
2. Salt crystals are larger and heavier than pepper flakes, and the static electricity is only strong enough to lift the smaller crystals.

MiniLAB (page 4)
In one possible circuit, the wire is attached to the negative terminal of the battery and to the side of the lightbulb. When the base of the lightbulb touches the positive terminal of the battery, the bulb lights.

Lab (page 5)
Lab Preview
1. Students should wear safety goggles because they will be handling glass lightbulbs.
2. The highest number of bulbs will be three.

Conclude and Apply
1. The brightness of each bulb didn't change as more bulbs were added.
2. The current in each bulb didn't change as more bulbs were added.

Lab (page 7)
Lab Preview
1. eye safety, clothing protection
2. volts (V)

Conclude and Apply
1. Student graphs should indicate that flow rate increases as height increases.
2. As the diameter of the tube decreases, the rate of flow of the water decreases.
3. The height of the funnel corresponds to voltage.
4. The diameter of the tube corresponds to resistance.
5. As voltage increases, the current increases.
6. As resistance increases, the current decreases.

Laboratory Activity 1 (page 9)
Data and Observations
Table 1
1. Predictions will vary; bulbs light; bulbs light
2. Predictions will vary; bulbs light; bulbs light
3. Predictions will vary; bulbs light; bulbs light
4. Predictions will vary; no change; no change
5. Predictions will vary; bulbs light; bulbs light
6. Predictions will vary; bulbs light; bulbs light
7. Predictions will vary; bulbs light; bulbs light
8. Predictions will vary; no change; no change
9. Predictions will vary; no change; no change
10. Predictions will vary; no change; no change
11. bulbs light on either initial or reversed connection

Questions and Conclusions
1. The list should include aluminum foil, brass screw, copper pipe, graphite, nail, paper clip, and sometimes a diode.
2. The list should include glass rod, plastic pen cap, rubber eraser, wooden stick, and sometimes a diode.
3. The diode appeared in both lists.
4. The bulbs light due to current in the circuit.
5. Students should have observed that all metal materials conducted well.
6. Graphite is a nonmetal.
7. Plastics, glass, wood, and rubber make good insulators.
8. A diode could be used to ensure that a current runs in one direction only.

Laboratory Activity 2 (page 13)
Data and Observations
Table 1
1. no changes; 0 volts
2. some bubbling; Answers will vary.
3. some bubbling; Answers will vary.
4. no changes; 0 volts

Questions and Conclusions
1. The battery conditions with the copper strip, aluminum foil, and hydrochloric acid should produce the highest voltage.
2. HCl produced the higher voltage because it is a stronger acid.
3. Bubbles were observed, and a voltage was produced.
4. Copper and aluminum together produced the best batteries
5. Students should observe little change in the appearance of the copper strip, but the aluminum foil should show definite evidence of corrosion.

Meeting Individual Needs

Directed Reading for Content Mastery (page 19)
Overview (page 19)
1. circuit
2. Ohm's
3. $I = V/R$
4. the same
5. parallel
6. different
7. 3
8. 2
9. 1
10. 4

Section 1 (page 20)
1. I
2. C
3. I
4. I
5. C
6. C

7. I
8. I
9. C
10. T, It is repelling a ball with a positive charge because like charges repel each other.
11. T, It is attracted to the ball with the positive charge because unlike charges attract each other.
12. F, The positive charge of ball 2 will repel it.

Sections 2 and 3 (page 21)
1. parallel
2. no
3. 3
4. yes, bulbs 1 and 2
5. series
6. yes
7. no

Key Terms (page 22)
1. static charge
2. conductors
3. insulators
4. electric current
5. circuit
6. resistance
7. series circuit
8. parallel circuit
9. ion
10. voltage
11. electric force
12. Ohm's law
13. electric field
14. electric power
15. electric discharge

Lectura dirigida para Dominio del contenido (pág. 23)

Sinopsis (pág. 23)
1. circuito
2. de Ohm
3. $I = V/R$
4. la misma
5. en paralelo
6. diferente
7. 3
8. 2
9. 1
10. 4

Secciones 1 y 3 (pág. 24)
1. I
2. C
3. I
4. I
5. C
6. C
7. I
8. I
9. C
10. V. Repele la bola con carga positiva porque las cargas iguales se repelen mutuamente.
11. V. Se ve atraído hacia la bola con carga positiva porque las cargas distintas se atraen mutuamente.
12. F. La carga positiva de la bola 2 la repelerá.

Secciones 2 y 3 (pág. 25)
1. paralelo
2. no
3. 3
4. sí, bombillas 1 y 2
5. en serie

6. sí
7. no

Términos claves (pág. 26)
1. carga estática
2. conductores
3. aisladores
4. corriente eléctrica
5. circuito
6. resistencia
7. circuito en serie
8. circuito en paralelo
9. ion
10. voltaje
11. fuerza eléctrica
12. ley de Ohm
13. campo eléctrico
14. fuerza eléctrica
15. descarga eléctrica

Reinforcement (page 27)

Section 1 (page 27)

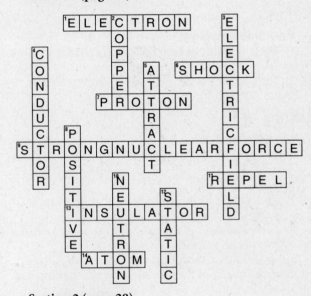

Section 2 (page 28)
1. electric current
2. circuit
3. negative
4. positive
5. electric potential energy
6. volts
7. V
8. chemical reactions
9. resistance
10. ohms

Section 3 (page 29)
1. a. Ohm's law
   b. Voltage = current × resistance
   c. $V = I \times R$

2. **a.** parallel circuit
   series circuit
   b. parallel: a circuit that has more than one path
   for the electric current to follow
   series: a circuit that has only one path for the
   electric current to follow
3. **a.** amount of electric energy used by a device
   b. watt
   W
   kilowatt
   kW
   c. power = current × voltage
   $P = I \times V$

Enrichment (page 30)

Section 1 (page 30)
1. All forms of lightning involve the attraction of
   positive and negative electrical charges. These
   interactions involve charges that build up in the
   clouds as well as the positive charge of the
   ground.
2. The lightning flash occurs so quickly that we do
   not observe the upward reach of the lightning
   from the ground.

Section 2 (page 31)
1. **a.** $(103 + 933) \times 0.13)/12 = \$11.22$
   b. $(190 \times 0.13)/12 = \$2.06$
   c. $(46 \times 0.13)/12 = \$0.50$
   d. $(440 \times 0.13)/12 = \$4.77$
   e. $(363 \times 0.13)/12 = \$3.93$
2. Answers will vary, but should reflect the local rate
   multiplied by each of the numbers in the chart.

Section 3 (page 32)
1. $R = V/I$ so $I = V/R$, $I = 160$ V/40 ohms, $I = 4$ A
2. $R = V/I$ so $I = V/R$, $I = 12$ V/32 ohms, $I = 0.375$ A
3. $R = V/I$ so $V = I/R$, $V = (28$ ohms$)(3.8$ A$)$,
   $V = 106.4$ V
4. $R = V/I$, $R = 3$ V$/2 \times 10^{-4}$ A $= 1.5 \times 10^4$ ohms $=$
   2×10^4 ohms

Note-taking Worksheet (page 33)
Refer to Teacher Outline, student answers are
underlined.

Assessment

Chapter Review (page 37)
Part A. Vocabulary Review (page 37)

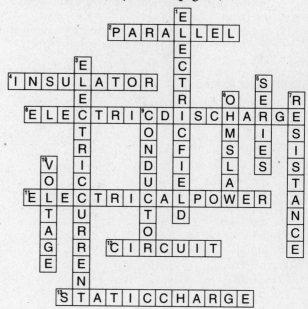

Across
2. (9/3)
4. (3/1)
8. (4/1)
11. (10/3)
12. (9/3)
13. (1/1)

Down
1. (2/1)
3. (5/2)
5. (9/3)
6. (8/3)
7. (7/2)
9. (3/1)
10. (5/2)

Part B. Concept Review (page 38)
1. loses electrons (1/1)
2. attract (2/1)
3. weaker (2/1)
4. neutral (4/1)
5. a source of electrons (5/2)
6. voltage (5/2)
7. separating (6/2)
8. negative; positive (6/2)
9. decreases (7/2)
10. ampere (5/2)
11. current; resistance (8/3)
12. 0.19 amperes (8/3)
13. current (9/3)
14. power (10/3)
15. kilowatt-hours (10/3)

16. Both circuits provide a pathway for electricity and can be used to run electrical devices. In a series circuit, if one item is turned off, the whole circuit is off. In a parallel circuit, adding or removing items does not affect the total circuit. (9/3)

17. It can cause the heart to stop beating properly. It can interfere with the ability to breathe, which can lead to suffocation. (11/3)

Chapter Test (page 39)

I. Testing Concepts (page 39)

1. d (3/1)
2. a (1/1)
3. d (6/2)
4. d (6/2)
5. a (1/1)
6. d (5/2)
7. b (3/1)
8. c (6/2)
9. b (9/3)
10. a (1/1)
11. a (7/2)
12. c (6/2)
13. d (7/2)
14. c (8/3)
15. b (1/1)
16. c (10/3)
17. b (9/3)
18. watt (10/3)
19. volt (6/2)
20. ampere (5/2)
21. ohm (8/3)

II. Understanding Concepts (page 41)

1. The cloth lost its electrons to the rubber rod. (1/1)
2. The rod has a negative charge. (1/1)
3. Charged objects exert electric force. (2/1)
4. The ball becomes negatively charged. (1/1)
5. The ball is repelled by the rod. (2/1)
6. **A.** batteries (8/3)
   B. closed switch (8/3)
   C. bulb (8/3)
7. parallel (9/3)
8. D will still be lit. (9/3)

III. Applying Concepts

1. $I = V/R$; $I = 1.5$ volts/0.75 ohms = 2 amperes (8/3)
2. 3 volts (8/3)
3. $P = I \times V$; $P = 4$ amperes $\times$ 3 volts = 12 watts (10/3)
4. The bulb in circuit B. When the resistance is kept the same, as voltage increases, current increases. Since circuit B has more voltage, there is more current flowing through the bulb in circuit B, making it brighter. (9/3)

IV. Writing Skills (page 42)

1. If lightning strikes the rods, they will conduct the excess electric charge into the ground where it cannot do any damage. (4/1)
2. Even a small amount of current passing through a hand can cause the muscles to contract very tightly. (11/3)

Transparency Activities

Section Focus Transparency 1 (page 44)

A Spritely Vision

Transparency Teaching Tips

- The concept of electricity is introduced here. Explain that every atom is composed of smaller particles—electrons, protons, and neutrons. Electrons carry a negative electrical charge, and protons carry a positive charge, while neutrons carry no electrical charge at all.
- Charges can be transferred, such as by rubbing solids together or when some substances are dissolved in solution. Atoms can gain electrons (and, therefore, become negatively charged) or lose them (and become positively charged). A charged atom is called an ion.
- Every charged object exerts an electrical force on other charged objects, (like charges repel, opposite charges attract). A charged particle has an electric field surrounding it. The closer to the charged particle, the stronger this field is.
- Lightning is caused by the electrical attraction of oppositely charged particles. Light water droplets colliding with heavier ice particles and other particulate matter within a cloud cause negatively charged particles to move to the bottom of the cloud and positively charged particles to the top. When these charges begin to move toward each other, or toward oppositely charged particles on Earth, an electrical discharge takes place. Lightning can occur within a cloud, between clouds, or between a cloud and the ground.
- A sprite, shown on the transparency, is the result of an intense lightning strike that creates a strong electric field above the cloud. Electrically charged particles in this field glow red as a result. These sprites only last 3–10 milliseconds and are very dim, making them impossible to view from a city and nearly impossible elsewhere with the naked eye.

Content Background

- Sprites were first captured on a light-sensitive radio camera mounted in a jet in 1990. They exist between altitudes of 65 and 90 km (40 and 59 miles), near or in the ionosphere, where the majority of particles are electrically charged.
- Sprites only occur with about one percent of lightning discharges.

- A strike of lightning may reach 33,000°C (60,000°F) and discharge 100 million volts of electricity.

Answers to Student Worksheet
1. Lightning is an electric discharge that can cause damage because of the extremely large amount of electric energy released.
2. It appears to be an electrical discharge. It's less bright, a different color, and less powerful.
3. A flash of lightning is a sudden discharge of a very large amount of electric energy. A lightbulb uses electric current, which is a steady flow of charge through a conductor.

Section Focus Transparency 2 (page 45)

Go with the Flow!

Transparency Teaching Tips
- This is an introduction to current electricity. Explain that the electrical energy that powers household appliances comes from a power plant in the form of an electric current. The current travels through a conductor, usually wire composed of metal, most often copper. If one end of the conductor is positively charged and the other negatively, energy in the form of electrons will flow through the conductor.
- Highway traffic flow, as shown on the transparency, represents direct current flow. The current moves at a constant rate in one direction, filling the conducting medium, in this case the highway.
- Ask the students to identify things that would slow this traffic flow. Explain that the flow of electric current depends upon resistance in the conductor. Materials with free-flowing electrons provide little resistance to current and, like copper wire, are said to be good conductors. Some materials offer some resistance and are called semiconductors. Semiconductors are used to control electrical flow. Other materials, such as wood and glass, have tightly bound electrons and inhibit current flow. Such materials are called insulators.
- Have the students explain why the exterior of electrical cords and plugs are made of rubber.

Content Background
- When electrons in a current collide with electrons tightly bound to atoms in an insulator, their energy is converted into heat. This is called resistance.
- Resistance varies not only with material, but with size, and shape, and temperature.
- Household current in the United States is not direct, but alternating. Magnets reverse current direction 120 times per second. This allows current to be sent long distances without cumulative resistance reducing it to nothing.

- Nikola Tesla, a Croatian immigrant to the United States, invented the technology that made alternating current possible. Although relatively unknown outside of scientific circles, Tesla was the source of a number of scientific inventions that significantly advanced the use of technology. Among his 700 patents are those for the telephone repeater, Tesla coil transformer, fluorescent lights, alternating current system, induction motor, wireless communication, and the radio. Tesla's work on the radio predates that of Marconi. The Supreme court granted full rights to Tesla in 1943.
- The word *elektron* is Greek, meaning amber. In ancient Greece, amber was rubbed to create static electricity, a concept not understood at the time. Our present understanding, however, originated with these early experiments, hence the choice of names.

Answers to Student Worksheet
1. It looks like there are too many cars for the road, and they are having a tough time moving. If the number of lanes were fewer it would be more difficult to get through. If there were twice as many lanes, movement would be easier by half.
2. Electrons move in a wire like cars move on a road. The more resistance there is, the more difficult it is to get through. Notice, too, how the cars flow around the island. The road is like a conducting material, and the island is like an insulator. Electrons take the path of least resistance through the conducting material.

Section Focus Transparency 3 (page 46)

In the Chips

Transparency Teaching Tips
- You may use this transparency to introduce the concept that electrons travel along pathways called circuits. The total amount of current in a circuit is determined by dividing the applied voltage by resistance. This relationship between current, voltage, and resistance is known as Ohm's law.
- Electrical electron flow can be routed in two different ways. In a series circuit, a single pathway exists between power source and device. Each device must pass the current along to the next, and each device acts as a resistor, reducing the current. If one of the devices doesn't work, the current is not passed along and the circuit is broken. Ask the students to give an example of such a circuit. They might mention Christmas tree lights or devices that use batteries.
- The second way electrical current is routed is in a parallel circuit. In this arrangement, each device has its own connected pathway. Should one device fail, the rest will continue to function, as each has its own connection to the power source. Houses are wired in such a fashion.

- The microprocessing chips of today's computers, as shown on the transparency, are miniature (micro) circuits containing enormous numbers of transistors that affect electric current flow. They are the memory and processing centers of a computer. The transistor switches electric current on or off or amplifies it.

Content Background

- Integrated circuits are, in most cases, made of silicon, which is overlaid and etched to create electrical current processing devices. The transistors, composed of chemicals such as boron and arsenic, are added in layers to the silicon base to affect the flow of electric current.
- Improvements in microchip technology have allowed for the creation of smaller chips. This has increased computer performance, as the speed of individual and connected circuits improves as their dimensions diminish (less distance and resistance to current flow). Cost has also decreased because the volume of needed materials has been reduced.

Answers to Student Worksheet

1. They reduce the distance that electrons flow; smaller circuits experience less resistance. They allow the creation of smaller, faster, and cheaper computers.
2. Answers will vary, but might include televisions, radios, compact disc players, video recorders, telephones, etc.
3. Answers will vary. Possible answers include lights, appliances, TV, CD player, etc.

Teaching Transparency (page 47)

Flowing Current

Section 2

Transparency Teaching Tips

- Use the transparency to emphasize the analogy of the flow of water to the flow of electrons.
- Use the transparency to help students visualize the flow of electric current in a closed circuit.

Reteaching Suggestion

- Work with students to draw a diagram of a simple electric circuit and have them label what happens in the different parts of the circuit.

Extensions

Challenge: Have students brainstorm other analogies that could represent the flow of electric current.

Research: Have students research the work and discoveries of Luigi Galvani, Alessandro Volta, or Nikola Tesla.

Answers to Student Worksheet

1. The water pump lifts water against the force of gravity.
2. The potential energy of the water is measured by the height of the pipes; voltage gives the potential energy of electric current.
3. Water falls out of the tank onto the water wheel, and the force of the water hitting the wheel causes it to move.
4. Electric current transfers energy through the flow of electrons. Energy from the electrons is connected to other forms, such as light and heat.
5. Increasing the height of the pipes would transfer more energy from the water to the water wheel. The water wheel would have more energy of motion (kinetic energy).
6. a closed conducting loop; from the negative to the positive terminal.

Assessment Transparency (page 49)

Electricity

Section 3

Answers

1. C. Students must read from the correct column to determine that the clothes dryer costs the most to operate each month.
2. F. Students can answer this question by reading the table. First, they must find the two items that are used for the same number of hours (air cleaner and box fan). By comparing the wattage and operating costs for these items, students should see that the correct answer is choice F, *more to operate.*
3. B. Students need to find the relevant difference between the color TV and the laser printer.
   Choice A: No, the wattage is the same.
   Choice B: Yes, the color TV is on longer, which means that it will cost more to operate it each month.
   Choice C: No, size is not a relevant difference between the two appliances.
   Choice D: No, the power company does not charge more for the electricity that goes to TVs.

Teaching Tip

Encourage students to be sure they have everything needed for a test, including extra pencils and a working calculator, if allowed.